Start

The Starters' Playbook

Satish Mehta

Words for Start

A summary of a lifetime of hard-learned business wisdom.

Ten years ago, we started a real estate business from scratch, right in the middle of the Great Recession. We have been very successful. We do not have long-term plans, skeletal expense budgets, immediately changeable, and no specific sales goals. Everything is based on opportunities now, with a very serious eye on where the market is going or likely to go.

We could have saved ourselves some serious mistakes if we had focused on some of the key issues identified in this book. Everyone said we were crazy to start when we did. So much for consensus.

A great and easy read. A lot of serious and pertinent food for business thought and dreams which can come true.

--Rufus Williams, Principal
Cardinal Point Management Group

It is easy to be overwhelmed by the vast amount of information accessible to anyone interested in starting or running a business.

Satish Mehta addresses the most limited resource every businessperson has— TIME.

This book helps the reader filter through all the noise to - "What matters?" What should you focus on right away, what can you put off, and what is a complete waste of your time?

Satish's writing style makes his ideas easily digestible. It provides a perspective for anyone to identify and tackle the wide range of topics that people in business face today.

Mark Kuperman, Chief Operating Officer
Revenue Management Solutions (RMS)

Many people dream of starting a business. Few carry through. Fewer still succeed after they start. If they only had better advice and mentorship!

This book is for dreamers starting the business ownership journey. It is also for business owners seeking sound operating advice. In his beautifully simplistic, common sense guide - "Starter's Playbook," Satish Mehta proposes a massive paradigm shift, a new economic framework enabling unlimited opportunity for those dreaming of creating a "self-owned enterprise." As new technologies create increased automation, machines are replacing humans. Therefore, as Satish suggests, "There are no longer enough jobs to go around." He believes that the future belongs to the self-employed. They will use new automation technologies to rapidly implement new ideas, create improved products, and meet surging market demands.

"Starter's Playbook" is easy (and fun) to read. Unlike the typical business guide that "talks at you," this book carries on a conversation with you. As I read the book, I was transported to Satish's living room, listening to his decades-rich experience while making relevant connections to my own past and thoughts for the future.

The strength of this book lies in its simplicity and honesty. Satish says things that many MBA professors are afraid to say (see chapter 1 – "Debunkings" and his views on forecasting/planning). If there is a weakness, perhaps it rests in its simplicity!

For readers desiring reams of detail upon detail, this book will leave you looking. For those seeking solid, real-world mentoring and lessons learned, read it before your competition does.

Dan Grillone, Colonel (Retired)
The United States Air Force

Words for Start

INTRODUCTION

INTRODUCTION

The new framework

This book is for those who never thought of starting a business, to those running an enterprise, for the die-hard entrepreneurs born to create and lead, and for stable, less intense business owners.

How about dreamers stuck in a rut of day jobs? They dream about getting paid for pursuing their passion. Yes. This book is for them too.

We identify ourselves with the job we do. Even if it sucks, a job gives purpose and structure to everyday lives. It pays our bills and makes us feel responsible. We also like to believe that the institution of work is relatively efficient in creating job opportunities and incomes.

These beliefs are silly and belong to the old framework.

There are not enough jobs to go around. Since the year 2000, the net gain in jobs is zero. The jobs lost in the last two decades are not coming back. Jobs that do come back will be robotic, part-time, or minimum wage.

Discard the obsolete context.

An epoch of economic change with radical outcomes is underway. It is an opportunity for us to adopt a new framework—other than a job.

"What is that new framework?

The fast-moving technologies have made the impossible possible. Tools that were out of reach are readily available and accessible – I can videoconference with the touch of a key. Distributed workplaces are replacing the central work environment—work from home or while on the beach. The platform business model has made the capital-intensive supply chain model obsolete in several industries—hospitality, publishing, personal transportation, to name a few. You do not need to own assets – buildings (Airbnb) or vehicles (Uber). Productivity is moving forward in giant strides.

Result?

You do not have to work 40 plus hours a week. Starting a business while keeping your job or doing a side gig is often sufficient to generate the required income. You do not need to raid your savings or beg for capital.

A self-owned enterprise is the "framework" that will define us.

Over the years, I have led five startups, four turnarounds, and one acquisition for large firms. I ran my own businesses six times. Large companies acquired two of my businesses. As a managing director of a Venture Capital group, I also helped several business endeavors.

Now I am an executive consultant and advisor to C-levels and senior managers. I am also an <u>author</u> and a speaker. I have a few things to share.

Let us get started.

Start   INTRODUCTION

DEBUNKINGS

DEBUNKINGS

Naysayers

"If you can identify a delusional popular belief, you can find what lies hidden behind it—the contrarian truth," Peter Thiel.

When you start something, you will often hear, "Don't waste your time. It has never worked. *It cannot be done.* "

People saying this are the naysayers.

Someone wanted to invest $10,000 in Alexander Bell's invention, the telephone. That, someone, asked for advice from the president of the Western Union. The Western Union president, at the counsel of an internal committee, shot it down. He said, "This invention is worthless and will never amount to anything...."

It is easy to say "No" and be dismissive of new ideas. But, in the end, there is a good chance the outlandish becomes standard.

The thrill of working at a large company is to do what most long-timers say, "*Cannot be done.*" Ask yourself, "Am I part of an organization focused on holding the status quo? Is this a place where I can do the "*cannot be done*?"

If your "*cannot be done*" is groundbreaking, not everyone will support it or value it (at first). You will almost certainly encounter a lot of naysayers, and they will jeer.

That is how you will know that you might be onto something. You may have found a building block.

Building block

Why do people write history? Why are the events and biographies recorded? Is it because they make a good read and will sell many books?

History's primary purpose is to teach curious minds to learn from others' experiences, failures, and successes, and not fail.

Some say that failures teach us a lot. Several people have written on the virtues of failure—it builds character, a necessary path to more tremendous success, and so on.

Do not believe it. Just ignore it.

If we try to learn everything by experiencing it, then one life may not be enough. You can learn from other people's failures but have no reason to embrace them. Other people's flops belong to them, not you.

If other people cannot protect their customer base, it is not your shortcoming. You have nothing to do with it. If other people cannot negotiate skillfully, it is their deficiency. If other people cannot move fast enough to adapt to new technologies ...it is their problem.

Another cliché is "learn from your mistakes." It has limited value. The only thing it tells us is what not to do again. *It does not show you what the best next step is or what to do next.*

How about learning from your or others' successes?

Now that is of real value. It tells you what works, and you can build on it by doing it again. In fact, you will most likely do it better the next time.

Focus on what works, the triumphs. You build upon your winners and not failures.

Success is the best building block.

Forecasts and plans

"Forecasts of $XXM in revenue in five years" is a shot in the dark. All longer than one-year projections are guesses. Waste no time on false precision. Focus on the burn and your path toward achieving definite milestones.

"How will you get the customers in the first few months or quarters? How will you bootstrap when starting out?" Details matter more than gross, unproven assumptions.

Typically, a few corporate managers work together to write a plan that no one without actual field experience can challenge. The process shields planning from the current market reality. Why? Such a method is past-driven and myopic. A plan must be developed from the bottom up. Only people with in-depth, intimate knowledge of the field can develop an effective strategy.

The way many businesses work with marketing firms has often puzzled me. The companies will engage a marketing outfit to execute the tactics. However, the company prepares strategy before the engagement without the expert knowledge of tactics that usually resides with the marketing firm!

Since planning is mostly guesswork, it is better to focus on this week, not this year. Make just-in-time decisions.

Figure out the best next thing and do that.

Big vs. Good

"Tell me something about your company."

"Well, we are a construction company with over 6000 employees."

"Wow! Nice!"

Compare the above with this.

"Well, I am a one-man band working out of my home." There is a pause, a smile, and maybe, "nice."

Why is "big" more impressive? Why is expansion always the goal?

Many giant corporations began as small, no-rules startups. Original team members are mostly gone. Working there now is the same routine every day. Often these large companies want to operate as small businesses for agility and flexibility.

"How big is your company?" It is a question that gets in the way of "How good?"

Walmart sells groceries at the lowest prices. It is vast, and it is everywhere. Customer service is nonexistent, and stores are cluttered.

Publix has superior quality, excellent customer service, and a pleasing store environment. It markets only in the Southeast states of the U.S. Should it also try to become huge? Will that make it great?

Are Princeton or MIT not excellent institutes? Will expanding worldwide and hiring thousands of teachers make them great? Nope. Not really.

So why is it that we are more impressed with "big"? Maybe the right size for your company is four people, forty people, or perhaps four hundred. It could also be just you and your laptop!

Growth involves people, expenses, rent, IT, furniture, infrastructure, etc. These long-term commitments make business complex and risky. Grow step-by-step.

For many, small is not just the beginning or stepping-stone. It is a destination in itself, as long as it is sustainable and profitable for a comfortable lifestyle.

Workaholics

Boomers grew up workaholics. They proudly narrate stories of all-nighters and sleeping at the office, killing themselves to get recognition.

Working harder and longer hours does not mean that you are more productive, far from it. It just means that you work more and end up creating more problems than you solve.

First, working like that leads to a harsher burnout crash. Second, trying to fix issues by increasing the work hours – throwing more resources at the problems—favors brawn over the brain. The most likely outcome is inferior results.

Workaholics are unlikely to make sound decisions consistently. They are so tired that they cannot discriminate between what is worth extra effort and what is not.

Millennials and Gen Z have made the cliché, work smarter, not harder real. They find ways to be more efficient. They grew up with new technologies and are experts at using the tools.

Bottom line?

The workaholics do not accomplish more than intelligent workers do. Of course, some of them consider themselves perfectionists. Most of the time, it means that they are wasting time on unnecessary details.

Workaholics are not role models. The actual role model is a Mom who finished what needed to be done faster and is now home taking care of the family.

Labels

"What do you do?"

"Oh, I am an entrepreneur."

"Yeah. So, what do you do?"

You see where I am going with this. Some labels are bland and meaningless. The title "entrepreneur" sounds as if a person is like a ship without a rudder.

Some people got creative and began calling individual employees within the womb of a large company "intrapreneurs." They are supposed to have entrepreneurial traits inside the corporation. Gee whiz. What the heck does that mean? What about the rest of the employees?

Forget the labels. Do what you love to do on your own terms and monetize it. That is called starting a business. I know people who do that and do not even think of themselves as entrepreneurs or business owners.

Stacy used to be a financial analyst at an insurance company. One day she just walked out and decided to do something she likes. During this time of introspection, she did a lot of Yoga and meditation to stay calm.

Well, fast-forward two years, she now has a studio where she teaches Yoga and meditation. Her practice has about 110 members paying an annual fee of $1,000 or more. Ask her if she is an entrepreneur or businesswoman. Her response is a simple answer, "No. I just started doing something I like to do and getting paid for it."

You do not need any sheepskin like an MBA or a technical degree. You just need an idea, confidence, necessary _communication skills_, and inspiration to get started.

BECOME

Start   BECOME

21

Meaningful

What is meaningful to you? What do you expect in return?

Recognition?

Access to prominent people?

Valuable content?

A sizable material gain?

Your customers most likely have similar wants—recognition, access to prominent people, valuable content, and possibly a material benefit.

The meaningful activity does not have to be a pioneering work like Uber that radically changed the taxi business. It could happen by your passion for helping seniors in assisted living facilities.

Your meaningful activity must genuinely make your customers' lives better. They must want it and will miss it if it were to disappear.

Problem solver

The cliché "scratch your own itch" has become the mantra of many business gurus. The premise is correct, but not without risks.

A problem can be of two types: existing products lacking the performance you need or a lack of products to do what you want to do.

In the first case, you are solving a quality issue. Products are there. However, for better performance, you may pay a higher price. In the second case, either the products just do not exist, or access is difficult.

In both cases, you know the problem, the current solution, and what performance factors matter. You can avoid much of the expensive research in building the offer.

If you start a business around performance improvement, the incumbents will strive to drive you out of business. If they have a significant resource advantage, you could be in trouble.

Dropbox introduced superior document storage and sharing solutions to an unserved, new audience. It avoided competing directly with the incumbents. That is smart.

Before starting a business around a problem, clearly understand whether your solution improves or is a new product. Grasp the competitive landscape and then design the best marketing strategy.

Learner Doer

Learning a new skill is possible. You can become a software coder, musician, artist, or author. Just start doing it.

If you are afraid to speak up, speak up a little every day. Not to the actors at the Academy Awards event, but someone. Simply, anyone. At a coffee shop. On the street. Anywhere.

The magic to creating something is to start doing it – taking action.

If you have an idea, act on it. Why? Well, what is the value of an idea without action? How much will you be able to sell it for? Most likely, not much.

Until you start making something, your brilliant idea is just an opinion. And, as the saying goes, "opinions are a dime a dozen."

Investors know that ideas are plentiful. A concept in the original pitch deck is a small part of the business. The real question? How well the presenter will execute.

"I had the idea for Amazon. If only I had acted on it. I would be a billionaire!" This is delusional. Having the idea for Amazon has nothing to do with actually creating Amazon.

Time maker

"Sorry, I couldn't return your call. Man, I am swamped."

Mostly, this is B.S. People call back or do not call back based upon how important you are to them and the priority they attach to your call. Rarely do they not call back because they have no time.

The same thing applies when you have to start or make something. If you want something strongly enough, you will make the time—irrespective of your other duties.

Making time, I am not talking about all-nighters or fourteen hours a day. I am talking about just a few hours a week. That is all it takes. Instead of staring at your smartphone, checking social media, work on your idea. You do not have to quit your regular job. Just begin working on your endeavor at night.

Once you start doing something, you will determine whether you really want to do it or just a temporary burst of inspiration. Nothing lost. You still have your job.

Then there is the issue of when is the best time in life to start something? Is it when you are young or older? Or, when you are less busy and not outright broke? Or, when the kids are off on their own, and the divorce is final?

Of course, the underlying assumption is that you will be around forever for that perfect time to arrive! The difference between life and death is just one breath. Do not time life. Make time.

Principled

Why do you want to do what you want to do? Most great businesses believe in a principle. They stand by it.

Be clear about what you are willing to struggle for and then charge ahead. That is how you attract loyal followers, die-hard fans, and evangelists. Take a clear and firm stance.

Some people will debate your position. Some will not subscribe to what you stand for. That is a good sign. If no one is upset by your take, you are, most likely, not assertive enough.

I write books—about 150 pages. Historical facts, real-life experiences, and anecdotes are the foundation of content. These books challenge common myths. If what I write is not acceptable to everyone, that is OK. I am willing to lose some readers if it means that others value my books intensely. That is how I set my limit - my line in the sand.

"The world is a bazaar—Life is a negotiation" is based on my negotiating experience worldwide. Several conclusions are different from run-of-the-mill negotiation books. Some authors claim that everything is negotiable.

Do not believe it. Try to negotiate somebody's religion!

Twitter stands for brevity. You must express yourself in 280 characters. Since its founding, it has increased the number of characters allowed only once – from 140 characters to 280 characters. Some criticized the change, pointing out amends they would rather see. But, there was no debate. Twitter stands for brevity.

In Tampa, Florida, Edward's Pipe and Tobacco shop needs no introduction to those who enjoy a quality cigar or pipe smoke. What is its line in the sand? Quality. Nothing but the top-quality cigars and tobacco.

When you are not clear about your "Why," every action is a suspect. But when you know what you believe in, your decisions are apparent.

Values leader

A bunch of corporate types meets and puts together a statement of company values. They wordsmith a paragraph that rarely tells a reader what the business is all about. They construct a list of mores that no one in the company cares about or reads ever again.

Ever seen the "best customer experience" touted by one of the largest banks in the U.S.? Does the bank really practice it?

Imagine hefty unauthorized charges on your bank statement. There is no way of reporting it on the automated response system. You have been trying to reach customer service for many hours. Your account page shows a specific number to call. Dial that number, and it takes you back to the automatic response recording.

While you are on hold, that recording tells you how much the company values you as a customer. Are you kidding me? If that is how you feel, then hire some more support people.

The slogan, "best customer experience," is different from the customers' actual encounters.

People in the company must know how to show the values of the organization. This is not the same as the leadership issuing a pocket card with a bullet list. The leaders must encourage the behavior to live the values

OPM Avoider

When thinking of starting a business, the first question most people ask, "Where is the money going to come from?"

My answer: "When you really need it, it will come from wherever it is right now."

Self-proclaimed success gurus and slick salespeople often promote using OPM (other people's money). This may make sense if you start an asset-based business, e.g., a hotel. Or, maybe you are looking to develop a vaccine for an incurable disease. You need highly qualified people to do the research. In such cases, you may need investors. But more often than not, when starting a business, the necessary capital is minimum or none.

I am a corporate consultant and an author. I work solo, so do IT contractors, project managers, marketing professionals, Yoga teachers, and hundreds of other skilled workers. They run their own shop— alone.

No matter what kind of business you are starting, avoid outside funding. It has drawbacks.

Losing Control

Debt or equity, the investors will have a
degree of control over your actions.

As a builder, I bought land and raised
construction loans from the bank. Anyone who
has taken a construction loan will tell you the
number of conditions a bank will insert in the
contract. Some of them will hinder project
efficiencies.

In other businesses, too, initially, it is
honkey-dory when all equity investors agree.
What happens if the economic environment takes
a sudden hit—COVID 19 pandemic, for example?
Will you be in your own business to take orders
from someone else?

Cashing out

In the mid-1970s, SEC further deregulated
the financial industry. After the change, the types
of people for the director and senior positions in
corporations changed.

Earlier, the head of an American company
was most likely an engineer or a major in
industrial management. They felt ownership of
the company and cared for the long-term well-
being of the business. After dismantling, most
came with experience in financial wizardry. Their

focus was short-term, and loyalty was to themselves. Maximizing the share price in the near term was their only priority. This is the "Wall Street" economy.

This is also the "Outside Investors" philosophy. They want their money back—and quickly (usually three to five years.). This focus to cash out rapidly almost always damages the longer-term health of the business.

Distracting and draining

Raising funds is difficult even for people who have successfully started a few businesses before. For a first-timer, it could become a full-time job. It could consume months or even years of meetings making pitches, and negotiating the terms and conditions. So, what happens to the actual business you are starting? It is a massive diversion.

Good deal or bad deal

The worst time to raise funds is when you are starting out. You are at the high-risk stage, and your success is an assumption. If you do not have a track record of starting or running a business, you are at even higher risk. You are not going to get a great deal.

Find a way to start your business on a shoestring. Before you make any significant financial commitment, get customers first. Focus on building what your customers want. Once you have customers and performance to show, you will have a lot more leverage in negotiating outside financing.

Let OPM be the last resort.

Ingenious

One of my mentees is a manufacturer's representative for the paper industry. After two years of hard work, he began seeing some positive results. He immediately wanted to hire one of his CPA friends as VP of finance.

"How many accounts do you have?" I asked.

"Six."

"Why do you need a full-time VP of finance or even a CPA? You sell capital equipment. There are not that many transactions. Just use Quicken or plain old Excel for book-keeping."

Whenever there is a temptation to expend money, one time or recurring, ask yourself,

"Do I really need this?"

"Is there a cheaper alternative that will be as effective?"

"Do I really need full-time people, or will part-time people do?"

"Do I really need a $500,000 construction loan, or is $200,000 (or $50,000) sufficient?

"Do I really need formal office space, or can I work from my basement? Can I share office space with someone?"

You can ask these questions for just about any business facet. Expend capital step by step. Tie investment to events or results.

"We will hire another employee once the revenue exceeds $10,000 a month consistently for six months."

Be ingenious. Many of today's world-class companies started in a garage or basement.

Starter

Many companies gather so-called high-performing employees and form a "New Business Ventures" organization. Within the NBV, there are teams and sub-teams, each leading a "startup."

It rarely works. The NBV organization is often a group of PowerPoint experts with readily available resources and no accountability. For them, expenses are part of corporate overhead, and revenue is an afterthought. All this while the teams are pretending to start a business.

The whole endeavor is too far removed from the realities of starting or operating a business. Revenue generates cash inflow. The expense is a cash outflow. Either make cash inflow higher than the cash outflow, or your venture is dead, period.

Corporate or sometimes equity-financed startups ignore this fact. They have no skin in the game. There is no urgency for turning a profit and be an actual, sustainable enterprise.

As a coach, I have heard some say, "Oh! Let us do this. We will worry about making it profitable later." These people are delusional. A venture without a clear path for profit is not a business. It is a daydream.

Do not be a corporate startup. Start an actual business. Worry about bills, payroll, customers, and profit from day one.

Builder

As a managing director at a venture capital firm, I reviewed numerous business plans and listened to many pitch deck presentations. The majority of them included an exit strategy.

Strange! Isn't it?

You are just starting out. Why are you thinking about exiting the business? Why aren't you focusing on building a company that will last? I would rather see the commitment to customer acquisition, retention, and resource allocation strategies instead.

Define your business vision. No, no. I am not talking about a To-Do List, a five-year plan, or a mission statement. I am referring to a real vision. What do you, as a founder, see when you plant one foot in the present and then lean out and place the other in the future in the "what could be?" The time horizon must be short, about three years, enough to be realistic and achievable, yet long enough to realize innovative and expansive ideas.

So, why do many investment seekers include "Exit Strategy" in their plan? They begin with the mindset of getting acquired. As a result, their emphasis is on the wrong things. And, what are the odds of getting acquired? Maybe 1 in 100,000?

What if your business does get acquired? What now? Spend one year or maybe two going around the world? Then what? Retire and play golf for the rest of your life?

That is why you see so many business owners and professionals retire for maybe one year and then get back into the game. Most of the time, they are back with a business that is not nearly as fulfilling as the first one.

If your business is doing well, keep going. Expand, diversify, and keep on changing. Why let your business be the one that got away?

MOVING FORWARD

MOVING FORWARD

Stay light. No, even lighter.

Starting out, a business is small, lean, and nimble. It is like a speedboat. Then, you begin collecting stuff, tangible and intangible. You become a yacht, soon to become a cruise ship.

The bigger you get, the more energy you need to keep moving or change direction. What makes a business heavy?

- Long-term commitments—leases, contracts.
- Excesses – overhead, people.
- Inflexible decisions—buy versus rent, salaries versus contracts.
- Meetings without productive agendas
- Bureaucratic processes and office politics
- Too much stuff—material, goods, assignments
- Overemphasis on long term planning

This is not a complete list, but you get the idea.

The more difficult it is to make a change, the less likely that you will do it. If you stay light, you can swiftly change the business model, marketing messages, feature set, and priorities. You can make course corrections. Essentially, you can change your mind.

Embrace Limitations

We know the cliché "necessity is the mother of invention." History presents plenty of examples of it.

For several years, Twitter allowed only 140 characters in a tweet. The users became quite adept at writing succinct yet impactful messages. At present, an average tweet is 33 characters!

How about the daily activities of people in many developing countries? In the U.S., we dispose of most stuff after a single use. People in emerging economies devise creative reuses. Pajamas become shorts. Worn out the toothbrush used to draw the string in the pajamas.

I am an author. I put a page limit on my books to force expression succinctly.

Listen to the great poets. They consistently put limits to stimulate creativity.

Leverage limitations to stimulate creativity.

Quality without Creep

Watch out for the feature creep in your offer. Keep a laser focus on few key features and do an outstanding job. Those will be your "talkable difference" to present in 30 seconds or less. There are not enough resources, time, and skills to do all things at once and do them well.

Most of the great ideas look great at the moment. Once you give them more thought and discuss them with a few specialists, they may not be that attractive or feasible. If they are genuinely unique and appealing, you can do them later.

Most compact things are more attractive. Think books. Writers sometimes cut many pages they love. Why? To write a great book. The same practice is used in making movies, composing music, and making speeches.

Chop off the fluff. It may mean removing some of the stuff that you really like. You are better off with a few great features than with a crappy offer with all extras.

Make core the best

What is the most fundamental thing that your enterprise will offer?

Hint: It is something without which you do not have a business.

Let's say you are starting a car rental business. You could think about a water bottle in every car, the cleanliness, an app for reservations, quick pick up and return, the company slogan, attractive facility, and so on. But first, you have to have cars. The cars are the core of your business.

Discovering the core of your business is simple. Answer the question, "If I eliminated this item, would what I am selling still be there?" A car rental company is not a car rental company without cars. You can take away the reservations app, the water bottle, etc. Some prospects may not like that, but you will still have a car rental business. But, without cars, no business.

What is your core? Which part of your business can't be removed? Find it, and then apply the maximum energy to make it the best.

Ignore the details early on

The investors moved from seeing lengthy business plans to about fourteen slide pitch decks. They like to know the "Why and What" first and worry about the "How" and details later.

Ever built a house? When designing a home, the architect and the homeowner concentrate on the floor plan before thinking about the brick or vinyl exterior, tiles or wood floors, and various appliance brands. These details can wait.

I use two or three PowerPoint slides in my consulting practice to make a recommendation. Of course, my preference is to cover it on one page. Why? Because at an early stage, my goal is to get the buy-in on the concept. We can figure out the details if the basic idea gains traction.

Most of the time, we do not know sufficient meaningful details until we start executing. That is the time for attending to the specifics.

Make swift decisions

When you have a choice between "let's give it some more thought" and "let's decide this now," choose the latter. This is true for everyday decisions, as well as many strategic choices. Often there is no need to wait for complete information or a perfect solution.

Every day decisions are like links in a chain. Every time you decide, you are adding another link and making progress towards completing the chain. The finished chain is your objective.

What happens when that unwanted email shows up? You have a choice. Either respond with the best possible answer or bury it in some never-used folder. Will the issue or problem go away? Most likely not. You may ignore it, throw it out, or sometimes deal with it later in haste.

Be agile, not hasty. When swift, we do not abandon our senses or our responsibility. We just leave the fear of failure. This is the only way you can pursue the work with a sharp focus, tenacious execution of the task, and nothing else.

Later, there is time to improve, add more features, maybe retreat and adjust. However, once you have the solution to a nagging problem, decide, please. Leave fear.

For many years, a small marketing services company avoided installing a customer referral program. There was no need. The competition was limited, and the size of the niche market did not attract more prominent players.

The COVID crisis led to rapid growth in the use of online capabilities. The more significant players with the platform business model can now address and service niche markets profitably.

Moving from a traditional business model to the platform model, the perfect solution was too big a leap and complicated. The leadership asked, "What can we quickly do right now that will bring results in the short term and be consistent with a step-by-step investment strategy?" The answer: Install a simple and sharply focused Referral Engine. The leadership made the decision in a one-hour meeting.

The company will eventually move towards the perfect solution. That is a big part of this. You do not have to live with a decision forever. If you make a mistake, you can change course later.

Be Patient when making change

Have you noticed a caravan? Everyone is moving in a herd-like manner. It is easy, safe, and predictable.

But, moving in a group, you lose your capacity to change. Why? Because you are going on a set, familiar path. Many will resist even relatively minor changes. A change means making an effort to learn.

If you do something groundbreaking, not everyone will understand or value it (at first). Your work has a purpose and is for someone—not everyone. Unless you are surrounded only by your specific audience, you will almost certainly encounter "everyone." And when you do, "everyone" will make fun of.

Whether a change is minor or significant, many will resist. If you believe in it, be patient. Over time, people will adjust. They may even begin liking it more than the old ways.

Keep it simple

Google placed a simple rectangle for search. Write or ask anything. It will fetch the relevant information. Other search engines had their websites crammed with everything.

Google won.

Ever watch a musician composing a song? Lyrics matter. It is not what a great musician included in the lyrics; it is what she left out. Authors and artists use the same principle – merciless removal for simplicity.

Just prune it down until you are left with only the essentials. Then repeat the process.

Edward's Pipe and Tobacco is one of Tampa's most liked places to chill and smoke a pipe or a cigar. It got that way because the owner thinks of himself as a curator. He is not just filling the humidor and the shelves. He is keeping only top quality in everything the place offers.

There is a reason for every cigar and pipe tobacco he sells: He believes each is great. He has visited the tobacco plantations and cigar factories and observed the ingredients and processes. He can vouch for each cigar and pipe tobacco's authentic flavor.

Look at how the owner describes a new cigar on the company Facebook page:

New to our Humidor. The RP Winter Collection 2020. Highlighted by a Mexican San Andres wrapper, Nicaraguan Binder, and Honduran and Nicaraguan fillers. The cigar is available in 3 sizes Robusto, Toro & Sixty. Production is handled by Rocky Patel's Tabacalera Villa Cuba S.A. (TAVICUSA) factory in Estelí, Nicaragua. Great Medium Bodied Smoke that will please all palates.

Everything we do has a mission, and if it is done simply, the job will be done well, and the product will be of high quality.

Better, not more

Cluttered websites rarely convert as quickly as straightforward, intuitive websites. Many companies think that offering a whole lot more will broaden the appeal. Instead, you end up with a messy site and a confused visitor.

Ever visited some old-style diners with an extended menu and about a hundred items? They have everything. Rarely anything is beyond ordinary.

If you want a great steak in Tampa, you go to Terra Gaucha Brazilian Steakhouse. They have a few items on the menu, all prepared superbly.

Large corporations use teams of people to design product features. The teams spend a lot of time to agree on the outcome. If the project is late, the company will allocate more people and money. Does it shorten the product realization time? Nope. It just makes the problem bigger.

Best to have a lean team with limited resources. Launch the product with a laser focus on what is essential. Trim it down and then polish it.

If you begin pushing back deadlines, you will never stop, and agile competitors will eat your lunch.

Focus on evergreen

As technologies and trends evolve, there will be new opportunities. Capitalize on these opportunities without compromising on things that people will always want—the evergreens.

Toyota's focus on core values does not change. Toyota vehicles are reliable, affordable, and practical. Its slogan, "Let's go places," conveys its values. People will always want these features.

Walmart focuses on low prices, big stores, convenient locations, and quick checkouts. Walmart stores have a user-friendly website for placing an order and prompt curbside pickup. People will always want these things.

Build the core of your business around the things that won't change—the evergreens that never go out of style. Avoid the fads.

Show your rhythm

A famous Indian saying, "those not skilled at dancing, claim the floor crooked."

I have seen dancers who have rhythm. You can see them dancing smoothly, even with crappy music. The rhythm is in their head.

Then there is me. You can play any music in the world. I will still be out of sync.

When seeking funding, many entrepreneurs present reams of data and hockey stick growth projections. They have little or no idea how they will acquire the first few customers.

You can also see this in businesses that spend a ton of money on the website, getting stuck on how fancy it should be – the colors, the style, picture quality, etc. Fancy websites rarely convert as well as straightforward websites with helpful content.

Use whatever you already have or can easily acquire. It is not the apparatus that counts. It is using what you have skillfully. Your rhythm is in your head.

Avoid by-product myopia

I consult all over the world. My book, "<u>The world is a bazaar, life is a negotiation</u>," is based on my experiences. It is a "by-product."

Businesses hire me to train senior executives in negotiation skills. Training is another by-product.

PayPal, known initially as Confinity, developed security software. When it did not succeed in that business, it switched its focus to a by-product, a digital wallet later called PayPal.

Consultants don't usually think about writing books or training personnel. A security software company doesn't usually think about a digital wallet.

In your business, think about what by-product you could sell. Almost every industry has one that can be monetized.

Just launch it

Bell Labs was one of the most prestigious technical organizations in the world. The professionals working there were perfectionists. And that was the challenge.

Agile product development for quick market entry did not resonate with them. To Bell Lab's technical organization, all bells and whistles appeared standard features.

In introducing a product or service, two fundamental assumptions are the value hypothesis and the growth hypothesis. Once clear on these leap-of-faith assumptions, the first step is to build a minimum viable product (MVP) for a market launch.

Why market launch with the MVP? Simple. You can test the hypotheses with a minimum amount of effort, resources, and time. It will lack many features that may prove essential later. Gauge customers' reactions and let them tell us which are necessary and which are good to have.

There is a whole lot you do not need on day one. Build the MVP now and think about the good to have stuff later.

Start

In 2004, how was Facebook able to raise much money when its actual usage was small? The Facebook MVP validated the two hypotheses.

The users were spending hours on the social network every day, proving the *value hypothesis*. Its rate of growth in the first month itself was staggering. This was without spending any money on marketing or advertising. This validated the *growth hypothesis*.

Do not confuse this approach for skipping on quality.

The most prudent way to make something great is through iterations. Launch, Measure, Learn, and relaunch with more features that you know are wanted. Toyota entered the U.S. market with MVP. Now it has all the fancy features.

Start

EFFICACY

EFFICACY

Do it real

A junior manager spends weeks completing the product plan. The senior team compliments her for her excellent work. So, what is next? Nothing. No one is reading it. What the company actually does may not resemble the plan she so diligently prepared.

Business history is littered with plans, reports, specifications, and other documents that go nowhere. Why don't they go anywhere?

Remember the cliché, "a picture is worth a thousand words?" If you want the audience to get it, instead of explaining it in boring details, draw a picture, construct a prototype, play a note, or run a trial.

Remove the ambiguity.

Ambiguity gives the impression that all agree. In reality, each person reading it may just be interpreting it differently.

How do you get everyone on the same page? Do something that others can see, feel, or hear in real-time.

One of my client companies wanted to install a Referral Program for new business development. They did not wait for the program to be entirely laid out in a fancy document. They selected two prominent customers and gave them Referral Cards with the value proposition. As an incentive for the customers to refer their company, they invited them to be panel members at their next company convention.

The trial tested the concept with real prospects. The final program has more effective tools and incentives.

Begin making something real. Anything else is just a distraction.

Know when to Abandon

Whoever said, "*Live less out of habit and more out of intent,*" must have had a profound understanding of productivity and meaningful work.

Do you do something, anything, to keep yourself busy? Maybe you do it as a habit and for no particular reason. Doing something for the sake of doing it requires not much thinking. Doing a task with intent and reason involves thought.

Before doing something, ask yourself:

Why am I doing this?

Did someone tell you to do it? Will it help someone? Simon Sinek has written a book, "Start with Why." It is a must-read.

Am I solving a problem?

Have you and your audience often faced the same problem? Are you filling a gap with a new solution? Usually, when you ask these questions, you may find that it is just a make-believe problem. You are better off not doing it.

Is what I am doing useful?

Whatever you are doing, is it useful, or is it merely cool to do it? Useful lasts. Cool, not so much.

When smartphones came out, everyone was installing apps indiscreetly. More, the better. Now, users install an app only if they will use it often.

When electronic newsletters were a new thing, people subscribed to them by the tens. Now, people unsubscribe to "useless-to-them" newsletters by the tens.

It is easy to be enthusiastic about something and neglect to investigate its usefulness.

What value am I adding?

What is "value-add?" Often it is confused with adding more. More features. Complex features. More options or settings. There is clutter, and the user is confused.

The real "value add" is when your customer can get more out of the product than before without difficulty. The added complexity or clutter diminishes the value.

Google added frequently visited websites' icons below the Search box. It allows the user to go to the sites with a single click. This is a "value add."

When we keep the user in mind and add something, we are more likely to add value. There is no need to add something unless it has a real impact on how customers use your product.

Is this the most straightforward way?

If you aim for "good enough" for now, there is most likely an easier way. Most problems are usually simple to solve.

Am I setting the right priorities?

What is the opportunity cost of doing what you are doing now? Is there something more important that you could be doing?

Most well-run companies strive to optimize resource allocation and use. Setting priorities is vital for smaller outfits with limited resources. Spending excessive time on one project may mean that some other essential stuff is not getting done.

Do I know when to quit?

Do you have abandonment criteria determined in advance? A specification, agreed upon in advance, to quit working on a project or worrying about an issue if certain expectations are met or not met. Such criteria prevent the indefinite use of precious resources and reveal the true worth of pursuing a project.

The bottom line? Allocate resources to productive activities. Ask employees these questions. You may hear some fresh perspectives.

Oil and water do not mix

I know Bob. He never stays late at the office, nor does he take calls during his personal time. Yet, he is always on top of things and completes his tasks. What is his secret?

He avoids interruptions.

Interruptions and efficiency are like Oil and water. They don't mix. Interruptions break the continuity of work; you start and stop, never cruising.

Many people get up early to catch up on work. Others stay up late at night. Why? These are the times when there are no breaks.

Set aside a block of time for alone work. During that time, cut off phone calls, messaging, email, etc. Just focus on what is meaningful.

I am not saying that you should not collaborate. If needed, collaborate with the most effective tool. Often, you could use a passive tool such as email and save time.

Meetings are interruptions

Often meetings are feel-good get-togethers. Avoid them unless it is essential to meet, whether online or in person. Usually, email or other passive tools can handle issues.

If a meeting is called, request an agenda in advance. It compels those requesting a meeting to think. It gives you a chance to assess the importance of the items to you.

If you are calling a meeting, make the agenda laser-focused and time-bound. Send the agenda out in advance.

Prepare for the meeting. Remind others to come prepared too. Preparation may reveal items that do not require discussion. Simple information exchange using email may be sufficient.

On the agenda, address the thorniest issue first, "Eat the Frog." Stick to the plan. Note down the outcomes, action items, and the parties responsible for the deliverables.

After the meeting, send the meeting minutes to participants, ensuring that everyone is on the same page. Avoid setting up another gathering.

Jugaad will do

A telecom company CMO struggled with the technical organization to expedite a marketing system development. The technical team always strived for the perfect product with several bells and whistles.

So, what is the problem? Time to market.

In the hyper-competitive telecom market, quick market entry is vital. A delay could change the competitive position. Winning lost customers back is difficult and expensive.

The CMO convinced the CTO to come up with a "Jugaad."

"Jugaad" is an innovative fix or a simple workaround. Often with a bit of creativity, a team can make existing things work or create new things with minimum resources. The objective is to do it quickly with minimum effort.

Google placed a simple rectangle for search. Find relevant information fast. That is it. It got to the market quickly. It added other features later to make it great.

Toyota began manufacturing Corolla in the U.S. in 1986. Simple, reliable workhorse. No bells and whistles. Good mileage at a low price. Got to the marketplace fast. Made it great after capturing a significant market share.

When a "Jugaad" will do, go for it. It is far better than losing in the market because you have no solution. More often than not, you can turn the "Jugaad" into a great solution later.

When introducing a new product, entering a new market, negotiating a contract, or addressing some obstacle, select the "Jugaad" approach for getting the most out of doing the least.

Eat an elephant bit by bit

Desmond Tutu said, "there is only one way to eat an elephant: a bite at a time."

He meant that you could achieve overwhelming goals by steadily gaining smaller quick wins. Quick wins build momentum, which is inspiring.

Sometimes just starting a long-drawn, a large project can be intimidating. Thinking about everything you have to do is often overwhelming. You may freeze before taking the first step. This is the reason many people starting a business fall short of turning their dreams into reality. They try to bite more than they can chew.

Break up the large project into smaller tasks. Every time you complete a job, it is a win. Keep making quick wins, and you will finish the big project.

Make the tasks:

Specific

It's easier to work toward a specific goal (write 1000 words daily for my book) than work toward a vague one (write to finish the book).

Measurable

Suppose your main goal is to start a business. Break it down into smaller tasks – create a business name, register the company, set up the tax ID, etc. These measurable tasks will keep you on track and are quick wins vital for inspiration.

Attainable

One pitfall to success is making the quick wins too aggressive. Inject realty. If you are a new writer, set a goal of writing one idea, about 500 words, a day. Aim at becoming a published author before trying to be the global bestseller.

Relevant

Set goals meaningful to you. Working towards goals takes work. Select goals that you genuinely want to achieve to stay inspired.

Time-Bound

Put time stamps on your goals. This will keep you focused. If you don't set a deadline, you won't be nearly as likely to stay committed and keep the wheels in motion.

Eat the elephant – bit by bit, bite by bite. You will make possible what at first seemed impossible.

Cut your losses

The sayings "cut your losses" and don't let "good money chase bad" are well known in the real estate industry. These are also relevant to most businesses.

I bought a child care franchise. It was supposed to break even in twelve months or less. After trying every practical improvement, and two years into it, the business still was losing money. The natural instinct is to think, "But I can't give up. I have a huge sunk cost!"

Well, the sunk cost is "sunk." A better decision may be to cut your losses and move on. Ask yourself, "Is the additional effort worth it?" The opportunity was attractive if it was profitable in one year or less. With the additional resources needed, I could pursue other possibilities.

I have also experienced this situation in the consulting business firsthand. Let's say I think a task can be done in two hours. Four hours into it, I am still only a fifth of the way done. My ego tells me not to give it up now. After all, I have already spent four hours on it.

I may complete the task to keep my contractual commitment to my client. But repeating it without pricing and terms changes would put me into a "faux star" mode. The task was worth it when I estimated it at two hours, not twenty.

Define boundaries. You may decide that if anything takes you or your team longer than two weeks, you will seek other professionals to take a look.

Sometimes an obvious solution is right there in front of you, but you haven't noticed it. That obvious solution might be cutting your losses—that is, quitting.

Don't fall into the trap of equating abandoning to failure. At times, that is the most prudent decision. You must know when to walk away. Most likely, you cannot recover the sunk cost, time, or money, but you will stop good money from chasing bad.

Estimate shorter durations

At a venture capital fund, I listened to numerous pitches for angel funding. The entrepreneurs confidently projected $XXXM in revenue over three or five years, and of course, the cost estimates.

My response? All forecasts and estimates (including mine) are wrong. Five-year or three-year financials and projections are a shot in the dark.

My advice? Focus on the burn and your path toward achieving near-term milestones instead of false precision for the longer term.

Investors are more interested in knowing how you acquire the initial customers. How do you expect to grow from 5 users to 50 users? Over how long? And how will you keep them satisfied? Better still, how will you get that one large client in the first few weeks or months? Near-term details matter more than unsupported assumptions.

In daily life, how often are our time estimates accurate?

The dealer estimates one hour but uses the whole day to service my car. I counted on writing one chapter of my book in just a few hours. It took me the entire week to write it. Sometimes, it is the opposite. I scheduled eight hours for online negotiation skills training of six executives. It ended in about six hours.

Most of us suck at forecasting and estimating. Even with simple tasks, our forecasts are off. We can't be accurate when forecasting or estimating a few hours or days. How can we expect to predict longer projects accurately? Often, we are not just a little off--we are way off.

Break up your forecast and estimate periods into smaller durations. Instead of one six-month project, design it as six one-month projects.

Keep "To-do" lists short

Did you ever spend more time preparing a "To-do" list than doing the stuff? Hey, you are not alone.

There you are, all stressed out. You have a whole lot of things to finish. It is overwhelming, and you do not know where to begin.

Yes, we have all been there.

Numerous so-called gurus have written books on time management. Steven Covey's "7 habits of highly successful people" still ranks as one of the best, even after about thirty years in the market.

My solution is simple—make shorter lists.

You don't need to spend hours prioritizing the tasks. Your mind will do it for you. Just jot down what comes to mind in the first ten seconds. Most likely, that is your "most important and urgent" item. Then the next action item, and so on.

Ask yourself, "Which items can I easily complete in the given time?" You will most likely end up with two or three action items. The top item will automatically be the highest priority. Once done, the next thing becomes the highest priority. There is no need to label them high, medium, or low.

Often there is a tendency to do things that are not that important but are easy to do. Unless there is some glaring urgency, complete these items first. Why? Little accomplishments inspire and build confidence for the larger project(s). It is a kind of preparation for addressing the more tedious and bigger things.

Make small decisions

High impact, longer-term strategic decisions can be complicated and take time to make or change. Once they are made, the tendency is to continue with the status quo. Why? It is primarily due to inertia.

Ask baby boomers who are empty nesters for quite some time now. They complain about high property taxes but continue to live in a large mansion where they raised kids – now millennials and the ZGen. Oh! Yes, they often talk about downsizing. Why wouldn't they downsize promptly? Mostly Inertia—changing homes and moving is tough. The same applies to insurance and other longer-term decisions.

Instead, take baby steps. Make small decisions. This way, you will avoid making irreversible mistakes. There is no significant price if you mess up. Often, you can quickly fix it.

Making small decisions is not inconsistent with more extensive, ambitious plans. It just means that the most prudent strategy to achieve big goals is a small step at a time.

Writing a non-fiction book can be daunting. Recalling all my experience and researching what is already out there on the topic can take months, if not years. It can be overwhelming. So, my day-to-day decision-making hardly ever extends beyond expressing one thought on paper.

Attainable modest goals, when complete, inspire you to move to the next step. That is a lot more realistic and gratifying than some fantasy goal you never finished.

Now or later

The quotes by world statesmen may be confusing without the proper context.

"There is more to life than increasing its speed." – Gandhi.

"Never leave that till tomorrow, which you can do today." – Benjamin Franklin.

When you are faced with the dilemma of Now or later, ask yourself, "What will take me to the solution I seek?"

If it is now, do it now. If delaying is the right path, do it later.

The tendency is to follow the most straightforward and comfortable path. But, almost always, the more robust way is the right solution. Follow what will deliver the best results and not what is most comfortable.

But, if you are inspired to do it now, do it. Why? Because inspiration is perishable.

COMPETITION

COMPETITION

Copy but don't plagiarize

"Nothing is original, so embrace influence, school yourself through the work of others, remix and reimagine to discover your own path...." Austin Kleon, author of Steal Like an Artist

People tell me that I excel at negotiation strategies. Then they ask, "How do you think about the best negotiating strategies?"

The simple answer is, "I copy first and then improve by injecting creativity into them."

Plagiarism is trying to pass on someone else's work as your own. Copying is about analysis and reverse engineering. It is like an engineer taking apart something to see how it works.

The mail-order business is not dead. Just the display, ordering, and delivery mechanisms have changed. It is now called "e-commerce." You see something on media – that is the stimulus. You order it online, and it is shipped to you online or via one of the several shipping services.

If you want to start an e-commerce business, you have to be selling a product or service. How do you find what to sell?

You have the same old mail-order business entry choices.

Copy. Watch what is being advertised online over and over again. Either the advertiser is nuts,

86

or she is selling and making money. Begin offering the same product or service. You may not make a whole lot of money, but it is the safer choice.

Of course, you could make cosmetic or adaptive changes to make your product more appealing. Just look around in any industry—auto, hospitality, fast food, and so on—the same product with a slight change.

Your second choice is coming up with something novel. With the proper marketing, you could do well, at least initially. Success does not go unnoticed. Copycats with a slight twist will show up. On the other hand, if the product or service does not catch on, your losses could be significant, both money and time. This is the risk of introducing something novel.

To copy successful ideas is to understand the needs, wants, and requirements to fulfill them better. Suppose you blatantly mimic a product without understanding the concept or motive behind it. In that case, your offer will never be anything more than a knockoff.

Inject you in your business

No matter what your business is, you will have competitors. Some will offer an exact copy of your work. Others may make a few changes. How do you protect your work?

Inject "You" into your business.

I know a consultant who is in great demand by C-levels at several large companies. His secret? Getting involved. Know everything about the client's business. Understand the client's customers, suppliers, competitors, owners, and processes. The C-levels know that he is no "armchair" general.

Investors always look for a competitive advantage (an unfair advantage) when funding a business. Often injecting "You" into your business gives you that "unfair" advantage.

Attack weakness in strength

Imagine an Indian car, Maruti, crashing into a Ford bus in a head-on collision. Outcome? A bus with a scratched bumper and an Indian flatbread—Chapatti!

The same thing happens when businesses compete head-on. A company with a lot more resources is likely to win.

So, how do you go against a company with a significant resource advantage?

Look for *vulnerabilities of* your larger competitors. Find and a*ttack the inherent weakness in the competitor's strength.*

"Rent Avis. The line at our counter is shorter." Long lines were a weakness inherent in Hertz's position as the largest rent-a-car company.

Auto rental companies invest millions in fleets. The hospitality industry invests huge capital in buying real estate. In both cases, the capital requirement is a significant barrier to entry and, therefore, the current players' primary strength.

Enter Uber and Air B-n-B. With a platform business model, they leverage the "sharing economy." There is no need for considerable capital. They attacked an inherent weakness in incumbents' primary strength.

But, be aware of weak points that are just that and not an inherent part of leaders' strength. Is the lack of live support an intrinsic weakness of Bank of America? Nope. BOA has the margins for a higher support level but no compelling reason.

No matter how good a new business is in a particular capability, it is tough to win if that is also the leader's strength. When an opportunity shows up, attack a flaw in the leader's power, not in its fault.

Attack narrowly

A marketing attack is an option for a smaller player to launch a *sustained* program against the leader. The trick is to apply significantly more resources sharply focused at the point of the clash. Gain superiority in the specific product or service in a distinct segment.

A team that attempts to gain market share quickly by launching aggressive marketing on a broad front is likely to lose most gains and then some.

Flank attack

A flank attack's big idea is to fracture the competitor's hold and create a momentum difficult for the competitor to stop. How well you do this will depend upon,

- *How well you differentiate your offer.* Your audience must see you as different and unique.
- *Where you launch the flank attack.* A flank move must be into an open or a relatively neglected area. Why? Well, we don't begin eating hot soup from the center. It is sizzling there. You do not flank attack at the stronghold of the competitor. Enter and occupy the undefended market first.
- *How well you keep the tactical surprise element.* The successful flank attacks are unexpected. The bigger the surprise, the longer it will take the competitor to respond. The surprise element also demoralizes the competitor.

The taxi, trains, and auto rental companies paid little or no attention when Uber entered the market quietly. Later, they were shell-shocked to watch the service grow at such an unprecedented rate.

Sometimes, the absence of an established market is challenging for the B-school types. The question often asked is, "where will the business come from?"

Usually, it comes from the incumbents, whose positions you are flanking.

When Uber and Air BnB flanked the transport and lodging industries, what was the market for shared economy services? They took the business away from the incumbents.

Test marketing can reveal your strategy to the competitors. It also presents a paradox. If it fails, it fails. If it succeeds, it alerts the competitor to take the steps necessary to ensure failure when the market test is scaled.

Stay in stealth mode but assume that the competitors will find out and have a contingency plan ready.

Reinforce successes

Your new product market entry is a success. The initial results prove the enormous sales potential. It is time to shift the resources to a product that is not doing well. Right?

Wrong! Big mistake. Reinforce the winner by investing more into it. Stop chasing a loser or maybe a would-be winner.

The idea is to reinforce the likely successful products and services continuously. Think of the principle used in the stock market investing, cut your losses and let the winners win big.

The best time to build and cement a market position is in the beginning when the new product is exciting, and the competition is caught off-guard. The advantageous position will not last long.

The big flanking successes of the last few decades—Amazon, Uber—all spent heavily "up-front." Rapid market entry and expansion are vital to prevent the leader from flooding the market with me-too products. What if you do not have the resources to reinforce the launch of a successful flank attack?

Remember People's Express—the first low-priced, no-frill airline? Disappeared. Perhaps instead of flank marketing, you would have been better off with Guerrilla marketing.

Flank openings

Price

You can enter the market at a lower price. The idea is to cut costs in areas not affecting the customers to a point where they will go away. In the airline industry, Frontier and Spirit do this.

Then there is flanking at a *higher price.*

In the 1980s, a cable TV technician used a field strength meter, a single trick pony, to check the signal reliability. Kay Elemetrics repositioned its spectrum analyzer to replace the field strength meter. The spectrum analyzer gave a lot more data with greater accuracy. It took the industry by the storm, even though it was almost four times more expensive.

I prefer a high-price strategy for three reasons. First, people equate quality with the price —"you get what you pay for." The second is the perceived status. Jaguar had quality problems, yet, it sold well because it projects a unique position. My favorite is reason number three—the potential for a higher margin, which allows the flanking effort's financing.

Size

In the nineteen sixties, GM and Ford made only big cars. Volkswagen launched the Beetle, a small car. The younger generation loved the Beetle, which became a roaring success. Thinking small made Volkswagen big.

Delivery

Amazon is the delivery-based flank attack of all time. Before Amazon, I went to a bookstore to buy a book. I could also order books through the mail. To see the readers' reviews, I could check newspapers or magazines.

Today, I can do all that, plus a lot more on Amazon. Why couldn't large bookstores compete? Amazon devoted overwhelming resources for the rapid expansion of the new delivery channel— online bookstore-- and stuck with it.

Segmentation

The consumer goods companies flank attack by focusing on a particular dimension of a demographic segment. There is clothing for short people, tall people, skinny people, and fat people. Duluth Trading Company specializes in "durable, high quality" underwear for working people.

Simplicity

Consumer Cellular partners with AARP to offer a simple telephone plan for seniors. It leaves out the fancy apps most seniors do not use.

Focus on creativity

Reiss and Trout's core message in the book "Marketing Warfare" is all about competing. All else takes the backseat. Other experts will tell you to focus on creativity and ignore competitors.

When starting a business, you don't need to be obsessed with trailing competitive activities. It is often a waste of time. Instead, emphasize creativity in delighting your audience. While designing a solution, if you need some competitive data, get that.

COMPETITION

GROWTH

GROWTH

Yes or No

Marketing gurus often repeat the cliché, "the customer is the king." For decades, the "king" appears to have contributed little to the inventions and paradigm shifts in society. Technical progress, societal dynamics, and business ingenuity have triggered the most innovations. So, how should you respond if just a few customers asked you to add some new feature?

You could immediately say, "Yes." You may end up committing to something that most customers do not care for. The new feature could take away from the simplicity and drive the price up. Nope. Not the best response.

You could immediately say, "No." An immediate "No" may tick off a customer.

It is best to take a break and give them a well-thought-out response. Be polite and explain the reason why it is not a prudent business for you.

Sometimes you can put a price on their demand. "If you commit to buying X number of units every year for the next five years, at $Y per unit, then we could consider adding this feature for you." Of course, you will make such an offer if it makes business sense.

Often the needs of a few customers change. Their businesses have grown. They now need complex products not attractive to most of your customers. Let these customers outgrow you.

Complexity discourages new customers who mostly prefer simplicity when starting out. Making changes to products for a few customers could alienate the broad customer base. Don't be everything to everyone.

Be true to a customer type more than an individual customer with changing needs.

Excitement vs. significance

Numerous Research & Development groups are teeming with ingenious developers and entrepreneurs. People there come up with ideas daily. Sometimes, they are really excited about the new thing. What will happen if these companies funded all or most concepts? They could go bankrupt.

For a long time, I had wanted to play the piano. I bought myself a top-of-the-line keyboard. I do not know how to read music, so I bought a few books to read music. I was excited.

The keyboard is lying in my study. I have no time to learn the newly discovered hobby. It was a fleeting desire. It would have been nice to practice, but it is not a high priority for me.

You will get many ideas from various sources. Some of them will be exciting. It is okay to get excited. It is often better to sit on them for a few days or weeks, or even months. Then, evaluate their absolute priority calmly.

An exciting idea today may appear so-so by the next day. Evaluate its real significance to your business and priority in terms of funding it.

Actual use excellence

You go to a store. You stare at a few products, and you buy the one that sounds like a great deal. It is a well-known brand with many features. The user manual appears to explain everything.

Then you go home and use it. It is not as easy to use as you thought it would be. It has too many features, and it is confusing. Suddenly, you feel that this is not the product you wanted. On top of that, you think that you paid too much for it.

What happened? Well, you just bought an in-store product. You are more excited about the product in the store than you are after actually using it.

Savvy marketers emphasize the opposite— something that's actual-use good. When you actually begin using their product, you are more impressed with it than at the store. The more you use it, the more you like it. And, of course, that is how word-of-mouth marketing begins – you tell your friends about it.

A simple product that performs the primary functions brilliantly may not look as appealing as products with all the bells and whistles. Being excellent at the core functions may not razzle-dazzle anyone. But that's okay. You want it for reliable, ongoing use.

In-store or In-media good carries little weight when compared to the significance of actual-use excellence.

Customers will remind you

What do customers want?

No need to keep extensive notes on what customers said they want. The customers will not let you forget the essential wants. You will hear from them time and again. After a while, you just won't be able to not remember them.

If there is a request that you keep on forgetting, that is an indication that it isn't that important.

Decide in present

Many business schools place much emphasis on long-term planning. But, the markets and technologies are changing too fast to plan long-term.

In about one year, online delivery's growth has surpassed the increase achieved over the past ten years. Online grocery grew over 30 percent in subscribers in about 20 days. Telemedicine, online education, remote working, and many more saw record growth. There is a big-time movement in trends that had been around before the COVID crisis.

Industries that are sticking to their long-term plans made years ago have suffered the most. In contrast, agile firms adjusting to the changes are seeing outsize gains.

Agility is the winning edge. Make decisions for the present and stay agile.

GROWTH

PROMOTION

PROMOTION

Embrace anonymity

When starting a business, keep a low profile. Stay in stealth mode. Test out your product or service in less known markets.

Why the secrecy? You can remove the kinks without getting many people to complain. The developers can make the necessary fixes, and you can streamline the processes.

Often, consumer package goods companies test market products in places like Cincinnati, OH, and Peoria, IL. You can fix the problems uncovered without upsetting too many people. The risk is low.

Once the product is out on a larger scale, millions may use your product, and thousands may complain if there is a problem. It is a much more difficult situation to handle. The risk is much higher.

Choose specific audience

How do you make your ideal clients Self-Select?

Get very specific about WHOM you address in your marketing. Choose a Specific Audience.

"Your Specific Audience is the sharply defined, select group you will focus on helping and being of service to."

Choosing a Specific Audience is all about focusing. WHOM will you speak to in your marketing?

Everyone has a Self-Label. In fact, each of us has several. A Self Label is a way we identify ourselves. The stronger the personal attachment to a Self-Label, the better it is for marketing.

The best Self Labels for marketing are so intense; people will defend them with vigor! For example, let's look at the Self Label, "Mother." What would happen if I went up to a mother and told her she wasn't a mother? I imagine she would be confused at first. If I insisted … she would probably get mad at me!

What about the Self-Label, "High School Teacher"? A high school teacher sees this Self-

Label in a piece of marketing and will say, "I am one of those! This message must be for me."

Strong Self Labels are black or white. Either you have kids, or you don't. Either you teach high school, or you don't.

Choose a robust Self Label to identify your Specific Audience to use consistently in your marketing. Your ideal client will say, "Wow! This looks like it was created just for me!"

A few guidelines for choosing a Self-Label:

Self-Label is binary

It will invoke a "Yes or No" response. A person will see the label in your promotion and say, "I am one of those." Or, "This isn't for me."

Lawyer, BMW Owner, Android User, Teenage Boy, Real Estate Agent are binary labels.

Person, Woman, Shopper are vague, broad, or ineffective Self Labels. Musicians and athletes are examples of labels where someone is not sure.

The more specific a Self-label is, the more advantage you have.

Use a Self-Label people use for themselves.

Just because you refer to some with a particular Self Label doesn't mean they also identify themselves with that same label. You might call someone a "Yuppie." However, the Young Urban Professionals might not relate to that. Using it won't get their attention.

If your potential clients do not use the Self-Label to describe themselves, you cannot use it in your marketing to reach them.

Choose ONE Specific Audience Per Piece of Marketing.

The rule is one Self Label per marketing message. Often marketers list a bunch of Self Labels in their marketing in hopes of not excluding anyone. They'll create messages like "ATTENTION: Coaches, Speakers, Trainers, Authors, and Entrepreneurs!"

Focus is diluted. People are confused. There would be an anemic response if any at all. Someone sees your list of Self Labels and says, "Well... I am a coach, but I am not a speaker..., and I am not really a 'trainer,'... but I am an author. I'm not really sure if this is for me."

If you have no idea what Self Label to choose, consider these methods:

Choose someone just like you.

Choose a Self-Label that you identify with. For example, I could choose a Male Writer of business books for myself.

When you choose someone just like you, you will know a lot about him or her because you are just like him or her. You will know what language to use, the content that will appeal to them, and where they hang out. You will have a good understanding of how to design your marketing to attract your client!

Pick a client you love serving.

Can you identify a Self-Label your favorite client uses? Suppose you enjoy working with this client and that your message is compelling to them. Why not choose to attract many people just like this client?

After selecting, create a client profile. Think of an actual, real live person that fits this label.

Next, make a list of everything you can about that person. When you think of a natural, live person as you write your marketing materials – you will write more intimately.

The clearer you get on whom you are talking to in your marketing, the easier it will be to write a message that feels intimate to that person.

Build the specific audience

Most companies have customers. Celebrity businesses have fans. But, the privileged companies have specific audiences. A loyal specific audience is their unfair advantage.

Many companies advertise to reach people and share information. It is expensive, unreliable, and wasteful.

Innovative businesses stress inbound "educational" marketing. The self-select audience regularly returns – to see what they have to say. This is the most receptive set of customers and prospects there is.

Build a blog about things useful to the specific audience. Track what they are interested in to come back to hear more. If they like what you have to say, they will likely buy what you have to sell.

When you build a specific audience, you do not have to buy their attention—they give it to you. This is a huge unfair advantage.

Speak, write, blog, tweet, make videos— whatever. Maintain a mailing list. Build your specific audience. When you need to get the word out, the right audience will already be listening.

Educational marketing

Do not outspend competitors. Just out-teach your audience. Make education the foundation for all of your marketing. Apply it to every item you create, whether it be a business card, brochure, billboard, or online post.

"Educational Marketing (EM)" informs and gives value before the prospect spends a single penny! It builds trust.

When you teach the audience something that solves a problem in their lives, you instantly build an immense amount of trust, which is the binding glue of all relationships! It does not matter if it is a romantic relationship, a friendship, a business partnership... or possibly a life-long association between you and your client! EM allows you to become a "Trusted Advisor."

Trusted Advisors bypass the typical sales process. They recommend it, and people follow it.

EM Focus

Suppose your ideal clients are all over the world. They deeply need your product or service. Here is something to think about:

"About 95% of your ideal potential clients are NOT looking for your product or service." Only about 5% of your ideal potential clients are actively shopping for your solution right now. They are now deciding "where or from whom" to buy.

Everyone with an even remotely similar product or service to yours will be marketing to this 5% group. They will be in a dogfight to get the attention of these active Shoppers.

About 30% of your ideal clients are simply not interested. They have the problem you solve but are not ready to invest for whatever reason.

The remaining 65% of your potential clients,

Could be open to your products but have not decided to purchase a specific brand.

May know that they need a solution but have not made getting one a high priority.

Either they may be unaware of their problem, or someone like you exists to help them. They are not actively shopping for you.

The #1 REASON most businesses FAIL is the dogfight for the tiny 5% of active shoppers! Their marketing is designed to reach 5%. They spend their resources trying to win the dogfight.

Effective Educational Marketing informs and inspires the vast 65% group of your ideal clients to buy your product right NOW!

Effective EM

"Effective EM" takes your ideal clients from simply being open or aware to being actively interested in buying your solution.

Most EM out there is not adequate. Some examples:

Free Evening Workshops & Info nights

Free reports

Tele-classes

Webinars

E-zines and Email Newsletters

MLM business presentations

The majority of this EM does not work. People may consume the EM but will rarely take the step to do business with the person who produced it. Why does this happen?

Well, helpful EM must have two elements. You must have both in place to access the 65% of untapped ideal clients.

Element 1: give value

GIVE VALUE refers to offering something of worth to your potential client right in your marketing materials. In this case, the value is in the form of content that solves a real-world problem (e.g., Top 5 tips, three Secrets, seven

Steps, etc.). This way, you include element number one of EM. However, this is where most stop! Do not. Implement element two.

Element 2: Position the Purchase

Positioning the Purchase refers to placing the content to persuade consumers to conclude that they need your program NOW. It sets the buying criteria.

Let us use an example of something I eat a lot of ... SOUP!

When you go to the grocery store to buy soup, you face a multitude of choices. How do you decide which one to buy?

Well, some people buy based on price. Some people prefer buying based on taste. Others select their soup based on the health aspects.

"Effective EM influences the criteria by which your potential client makes his or her purchase!"

Imagine you are pushing your shopping cart through the grocery store and see me there at a table, handing out educational reports. I hand you a piece that tells you about the hidden toxins in food these days. You read the information. You begin to realize the chemicals in food these days and what these toxins do to your body! How they can make your immune system tank – leaving you susceptible to getting colds and flu more often. Or, maybe they can cause you to lose your hair and get pre-mature wrinkles on your face! Yikes!

Was this report valuable? You bet. What else is true? As you head down the soup aisle, you are now far more likely to read labels and look for organic soups. The report gave value... but also positioned a purchase!

You must create marketing materials that give value while positioning the Purchase.

I am sure your business is more complicated than a can of soup, but the concept applies.

Tell them How

If you make chocolate, show them how. If you are a landscaper, show them 3D designs and the theory behind them. If you sell musical instruments, show them how to read music—even hold some free classes.

Show your audience the "What" and "How" parts of your business.

Just watch the shows on the media. The well-known chefs showing how to cook gourmet dishes. Hershey had a feature documentary on how to make chocolate and candy. Martha Stewart shows are famous for showing "how to" on numerous facets of household and family.

People are curious and want to know how things happen behind the scenes—why is something done in the way it is done. Show them.

What does it do for you and your business? In short, it develops trust and strengthens your relationship with them. They see real human beings, their efforts, and their bloopers and blunders. You are real and not Teflon.

Teflon people

You are most likely familiar with labeling someone as Teflon. It is a label used to describe those who try to show themselves as perfect in dressing up and talking. In reality, they come across as stiff, boring, and non-trustworthy.

Ever watched paintings of great artists? People pay millions for these works of art at Christie's auction. They are not a perfect representation of whatever they are drawing. But, these paintings capture and show feelings, emotions, flaws, and insights. They come across as authentic, genuine, and honest. They are clean but not sterilized—they carry music and poetry.

When something is too precise and polished, it loses the emotions and reality. It may become robotic.

Be real yourself. Tell the audience about your strengths and shortcomings. Engage them by inviting responses to something you are working on, even if it is not complete.

Sometimes, the audience may not see you as the perfect professional, but they will trust you more.

Releases are waste

It used to be that issuing a press release meant calling the reporters, meeting with them, showing them the newsworthy item, and convincing the media to write about it. The announcement was authentic, and the press was hungry for such news.

That was before the internet. Now an email blast to hundreds if not thousands of reporters is a piece of cake. The announcements are typically generic, boring, and meaningless. Journalists are bombarded with fake quotes from people they do not know. All senders label them as significant innovations and sensational breakthroughs—my foot. It is degrading.

If you want to gain attention:

- Do something different to make an impact.
- Do not spam. Develop a personal rapport.
- Call them.
- Write a private note.
- Contact journalists focused on your industry.
- Invite her to your works, expenses paid.
- Show her the new accomplishment with enthusiasm.

- Answer questions and explain the impact and workings in detail, if that is what she wants.

Be convincing and trustworthy. That is how you will get the best press coverage.

Broad publications

Unless you are a corporate celebrity, large publications have no time for you. Forget about pitching to a reporter. You cannot even get to him. You are too small to matter.

It is better to focus on media that caters to your industry. Trade magazines and niche bloggers, for example, will be a lot more receptive. You will get a quick response from the reporter, who is most likely also the editor!

The trade magazines and niche bloggers are looking for new information all the time. They want to be seen as trendsetters. Many reporters at prominent publications go to them to find newsworthy items. Often stories that appear in the niche media go mainstream quickly.

The trade media also delivers a better response in terms of leads and sales. Articles in major publications may help enhance your visibility, but they will not generate the same response rate.

Brilliant and addictive

Editing is a tedious and necessary part of writing. Contract editing services are expensive. Enter the editing software, Grammarly.

I began using Grammarly a little over two years ago. Initially, as a free subscriber. But, very soon became a premium account holder. Why?

The product is excellent. It lets me edit as I am writing, and not just my books or blog. It also edits my emails. It helps me develop the tone of my writing. Is it perfect? No. It is not. Often it confuses me with a "free" subscriber and promotes the features available to premium members. It is a minor inconvenience. I reboot it, and it becomes ok.

The product offers so much convenience that it is addictive. That is the idea.

Make your product really, really good – make it brilliant. Make it addictive. Offer free trials. Let the customers come back over and over again with cash.

Is this new? Nope. It is not. Eateries let you sample their food free—delis, ice cream shops, and pizza parlors are just a few examples.

In the nineteen sixties and the seventies, cigarette companies offered complimentary smoke at many events. They knew their product is addictive. Once hooked, people will come back for more.

Follow the same principle with your product. Make it so useful or enjoyable that it is addictive. Be confident that people will come back for it. If you are not convinced, you need to work on your product to make it that way.

Who is marketing?

The right question is, "Who is NOT marketing?"

The accounting department dealing with the customers and suppliers (invoices, credit terms, etc.) is marketing. HR is marketing to hire great people. Finance is marketing with easy-to-read reports for the investors. The technical department keeps stuff working for the customers – that is, marketing.

The janitorial staff is proud to do a bang-up job keeping the company premises clean and sparkling. Why? To make the employees, customers, and visitors cheerful and healthy. This is marketing.

You cannot put marketing into a silo. Every person, every event, and even system in an enterprise is marketing.

Overnight success

A myth among many entrepreneur wannabees is that many great brands got to where they are quick. The reality is different.

Almost all highly successful businesses followed a slow, steady, and controlled growth. They are not even close to the proverbial "overnight success."

The founders worked hard for many years before their firms gained meaningful visibility. At the early stage, most are no-name companies with products that no one has heard about. Advertising, promotion, or publicity will rarely speed up the process.

Great brands became great brands over time, without significant media or public relations push upfront. Amazon, Google, Facebook, Apple, and Dunkin Donuts all built their customer base over time.

Start building your audience. Let your audience hear what you have to say. Use the feedback to improve and keep at it. Who knows, in a few years, people may call you an "overnight success."

PROMOTION

HIRING

Learn everything

When starting an enterprise, learn to do everything yourself. Do everything yourself until it hurts. Then think of hiring.

One thing, you save a lot of cash. But, more important is that you learn to do most stuff yourself. This is a tremendous strategic benefit.

When you decide to hire, you will write a better job description because you know exactly what the job entails. You will see whether it is a full-time or part-time position. Is it a job that can be done remotely without sacrificing the quality of work? You will know the right questions to ask in the interview. You will also be an effective manager because you talk to people doing the work you have done before.

At times, you may feel that specific tasks are not your cup of tea. That is ok. You can hire someone to do it for you later.

You must intimately know all facets of your business. Relying solely on others is a high-risk scenario. Do not be an armchair general who is planning without the tactical experience of the battlefield.

Invent not positions

Hire when you must fill an open position with meaningful work. Do not hire just because someone with an excellent reputation is available. Suppose you have no meaningful work for the person. In that case, there is no need to invent a position with make-believe work and responsibility.

Hiring needlessly will just lead to a bloated organization. A whole lot of people will have no idea who the others are. The organization will be a collection of strangers bending backward to appease one another. Their output may not offend anyone, but the chances are that you will also not have a fan base – an audience that loves it.

You want a cohesive team where people speak openly and feel free to challenge an idea or project.

Degrees and colleges

How significant is a college degree? Does it give you what matters the most?

Many companies require an advanced college degree. Some hire candidates only from top-tier schools. Is this a trap?

Consider this. Most C-levels did not receive degrees from Ivy League or top-tier colleges in the top one thousand American companies. More received their degrees from state colleges than the likes of Harvard or Princeton.

Too much emphasis on academic credentials may not get you the most suitable. Take negotiation skills, for example. One of the most common traits of successful leaders is their ability to negotiate skillfully. Few colleges offer a program on negotiation skills as part of the curriculum. On the other hand, most colleges provide many subjects that help little in the real world.

In a nutshell, do not just hire people with college degrees and an all-star GPA. Consider community-college students, mediocre GPAs, or dropouts. They may have gained education with experiences other than in the classrooms. Discern between literacy and education.

Resumes and Curricula Vitae (CVs)

Most resumes are fake. Whether posted on job sites or delivered in an email (maybe a part of an email blast.). Titles are vague, and accomplishments are exaggerated. And the rules prevent us from conducting factual verification.

Qualified people seldom send out an email blast. They find ways to approach you in a personal or customized manner. Their passion and interest show up in their approach. No, they do not need to have all the technical skills listed in a job ad. They just have the right attitude, passion for the position, and willingness to learn quickly. They express these qualities in a cover letter.

A cover letter is a lot more revealing than a resume.

Years of experience

"I have 20 years of experience in ...."

So, what does that mean? Is it one year experience twenty times? Or, twenty years of experience learning all facets of whatever you are doing?

Most people take about one year to learn the terminology, the tools, and the way things work in an organization. After that, it depends upon a person's passion, attitude, intelligence, curiosity, and willingness to learn that make the difference.

I was talking to someone working in the IT industry. I asked him what he thought about TCS or Wipro. He had not heard about the top two IT companies in the world.

I met a young actress at Faneuil Hall Marketplace in Boston. I asked what she thought of the work of Martin Scorsese. She had no idea who he was.

I go to Edwards Pipe and Tobacco store in Tampa, Florida. The people working there can tell me everything about cigars, pipes, and tobacco. The types, brands, flavors, manufacturing process, the suppliers, the customer preferences, the distribution channels, the smoking etiquette, and the list goes on. The cashiers there do not have to know all that, but they do. Some of them have worked there for several years, others just a few. But, they all are passionate about what they do and curious to learn more. They have personalities of great employees.

How many years someone has been doing something is hyped. What matters is how well they have been doing it? How much more have they learned than the minimum requirements of their job?

Desks between doers

Who are at these desks?

They may have different labels. The common denominator is not adding any value, not when you start a business or are a small company.

They are the coordinators and the delegators. They do have a valuable role in large organizations. What do they do at a startup or a small company?

When you start out or are a small company, a small team, everyone is doing meaningful work. The team members know who is doing what. They coordinate themselves. In small groups, people know where each member is on the timeline.

Hire the doers, not the desks between the doers.

Self-leaders

Who are self-leaders?

The self-leaders lead and manage their own work. They set their own goals, timelines, and work hours. They do everything that an adept manager does to execute and complete a project. So, what is the difference?

They do everything themselves for themselves.

A Self-leader heads an organization of one. Once they know the desired outcome, the self-leaders need little or no supervision. Leave them alone, and they will surprise you with the amount of work they finish in a short period.

How do you find Self-leaders?

Dig into the applicants' history. How have they worked on other projects? Have they run something of their own, developed, or launched something? It could be at work or an extra-curricular activity. You want someone capable of taking a project to completion.

Hire self-leaders, and you will have more time available for stuff other than their supervision.

Soft skills are hard skills

One of the most common traits of successful leaders, professionals, or managers is their ability to communicate skillfully. Whether you are hiring a salesperson or a programmer, communication skills will make a big difference.

Why?

It is because being a good writer is about more than writing. Being a good speaker is about more than just speaking. They both must know what to say and how to say it. They keep the message simple and easy to understand. They know that less is more and what to exclude.

Writing and speaking are on a high growth path. People are texting, emailing, blogging, and posting articles on social media platforms. And podcasts and videocasts have gone mainstream.

Shop around the world

Thomas L Friedman first published "The World Is Flat—A brief history of the twenty-first century" in April 2005. The world had begun connecting a few years before that. It is essentially a connected world now. The advances in technologies have made geography almost irrelevant.

I write books. A professional in Mumbai, India, designed the cover for my book, <u>"How to be an American: An off-the-record guide for how to be an immigrant in America."</u> My editor lives in New Jersey. I live in Florida. Amazon does on-demand printing (somewhere) and ships it to customers all over the world.

Why not hire the best talent you can find and afford anywhere in the world? You want to see the team? No problem. Almost free video conferencing is available with a few clicks of the mouse.

Most professionals work on a contractual basis. There is no overhead, no long-term commitment, and most of all, they are motivated and inspired independent contractors.

What about the different time zones? Separate time zones improve efficiency; so long, we can manage a little overlap occasionally.

Melbourne, Australia, is sixteen hours ahead of time in Florida. When I need to speak with my team members in Melbourne, I call them at 4:30 PM EST, 8:30 AM in Melbourne. We have maximum alone time to do the actual work and remain connected in many different ways.

Geography is no barrier to finding the best talent you seek at a price you can afford.

Trial the hire

Many tout trying out a potential hire as a novel idea. It is not. Most companies make a new hire "permanent" after six months or one year. Full benefits and many other overheads do not begin until the end of the temporary status period.

You can test an employee on smaller projects and ensure the necessary fit in your company culture.

This has become easier in the gig economy, where contractual work is on the rise. Yes, I can test a graphic designer for my book's cover design without any commitment.

Stay close to customers

A personal products company had a problem. The sales of body powder were flat for three years in a row. All the customer-facing people were convinced that the product had no more room to grow.

An assembly line worker of the company attended a health and beauty trade show. He heard a common complaint talking to customers and distributors—the moist conditions clog the powder box's holes. It is primarily used in the bathroom.

He convinced his company to make the holes larger. Done. Bigger holes, more powder used. Powder consumption and, therefore, the sales increased exponentially.

No matter which organization, encourage people in your company to talk to customers. Understand what they like and dislike about your products. Some of the top leaders personally reply to the emails from the customers.

CULTURE

CULTURE

Instilling Culture

"Culture Eats Strategy for Breakfast," a remark attributed to Peter Drucker and popularized in 2006 by Mark Fields, the then president of Ford Motor Company. Many quote it. Few understand it.

History is littered with businesses whose well-crafted strategies failed. Many of them even hired high-priced consultants for help. Why did they fail?

Often they did not have the culture to execute the plan correctly. What is this culture? How do you instill it?

Culture evolves from consistent behavior. The leadership must encourage the behaviors they want to see in the company.

If you encourage people to make decisions, then decision-making will be built into your culture. If you reward courage, then courage will be built in—for example, the courage to make bold proposals. If you applaud innovation, then innovating becomes your culture. If treating customers right is of prime importance, then treating customers right becomes your culture.

The most significant thing is ensuring that everyone understands the expected behavior and people know how to consistently show the organization's values.

Own the problem

In 1982, somebody laced some Tylenol-branded capsules with potassium cyanide. Several people died.

Johnson & Johnson, the manufacturer of Tylenol, went all out to let the public know immediately. It explicitly apologized. It non-stop informed the public how it is addressing it. It led the industry to reform the packaging of over-the-counter substances.

J&J took ownership of the problem. Its actions were widely praised as an excellent public relations response to the crisis.

If something wrong happens, be transparent. Let the world know, even if people have not experienced it yet. If you do not broadcast, others will discover it and post it everywhere.

Where are you then?

Act like your customer is not trapped

Compare J&J's transparency with that of some large U.S. banks.

Competition is the driver for companies to innovate and strive for customer satisfaction. Unhappy users will move to your competitor. But will they?

Often, the cost and disruption of the move are significant barriers. The customer is kind of "trapped."

Large banks do not need to be customer-oriented. They seek to maximize profitability. Anything that automation cannot handle, they do not do. A customer could be on hold to speak with a live support person for the whole day and still listen to the taped lies.

This is the "trapped" syndrome. When the switching becomes cumbersome, disruptive, and costly, the objectives of the suppliers shift.

When you start a small business, engage in free-market competitive thinking, and when you have a "trapped customer base," act as you don't.

Propel your business

I called a local pizza delivery store. "I received your pizza about twenty minutes ago. I had ordered a pepperoni pizza. I received a plain cheese pizza."

"We are sorry for the confusion. We are sending you the right pizza immediately. And, it is free because of the inconvenience to you."

The store answered the phone on the second ring. They acknowledged the error and solved the problem promptly. Great service. I will order from them again and again and again.

Compare this experience with a Big Bank. I used Zelle on a Big Bank's online site to transfer money. It did not go through. Everything looked okay with my account and the recipient information. So, I called the customer service number.

(I paraphrase it below.)

"Your call is important to us. Please use online FAQs. If you want to speak with a customer service agent, please hold. We will be with you shortly." It is a canned message that plays on and on. And, you are on hold for, in my case, four hours, and still no one available to help.

These days this is what most people have come to expect from behemoth banks. That is why so many customer service queries begin with an irate customer.

Respond promptly, and the callers will love it. It is especially true if you offer a personal response. Everyone is so tired of canned answers. You will stand out by addressing the issue thoughtfully and showing that you are listening. Even if you do not have an immediate solution, customers will be happy with a response, "Let me do some research, and I will get back to you."

Prompt, personal response works wonders.

Build a great environment

Trust, autonomy, and responsibility result from giving people privacy, workspace, and tools they deserve. A great environment shows respect for the people who do the work and how they do it.

Treat them as professionals. Don't be looking over their shoulder all the time. The cost of constant monitoring is a lot more than letting people take breaks. May those breaks be for checking Facebook or listening to some Ted-Talks.

Let people strike a balance between work and personal life. Workaholics are not the most productive people. They may put in more hours but generally produce lower quality work and take a longer time.

The cliché, "if you want to get a task done quickly, give it to the busiest person in the room," is correct. They have things going on in their personal life. To take care of them, they do their job with efficiency, concentration, and focus. They finish their tasks on time to address matters in their personal life.

CULTURE

UPSHOT

Start

Just Start

In the nineteen seventies, people went to work buttoned up. Men in three-piece suits will remove the jacket and go around with the suit vest and the tie, looking like pigeons. A few, like me, went one step further. We wore fancy suspenders for the show.

The brand name consultants coined catchy phrases and esoteric concepts. To get a taste of this, read some of the business books written in the sixties and seventies.

The Teflon look and talks were supposed to reinforce the professional image. The whole façade was silly. There is no reason to emulate the absurd mask of professionalism that still exists at some of the large companies.

Leverage the greatest asset of a small company: simplicity. Communicate directly and simply. Reflect you. Carry out these practices in every part of your business communication—email, blog, website, presentation, and everywhere.

And, now you know the important stuff.

Just Start!

Start

Thank You for reading my book. Please leave a review of this book here.

If you think somebody else could benefit from reading this book, please forward the link.

About the Author

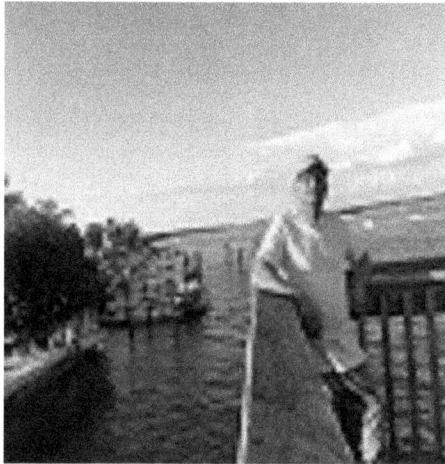

Still, a whole lot to write...

Satish Mehta is a consultant and coach for C-levels and senior executives of medium to large companies. He has held executive positions at global brands and successfully started self-owned businesses.

Connect with Satish:

LinkedIn   Blog   Amazon   email

Acknowledgments

Writing a book is never a solo work of one person. Numerous people have influenced me for over sixty-plus years. In that authentic sense, they are my collaborators on this endeavor.

Disclaimer

The contents of this book represent my experience, observations, and
opinions. No promises of income or results are stated or implied in any
way. Information in this book is not legal business or personal advice.
Many factors contribute to success in various aspects of the business,
including market dynamics, cultural differences, personality traits, and
sometimes just plain luck.

This book is neither a complete nor a most thorough presentation of the
subject. The views expressed are those of the author alone. The reader is
responsible for his or her own conclusions and actions. Adherence to all
applicable laws and regulations, including international, federal, state,
and local governing professional licensing, business practices,
advertising, and all other aspects of doing business in the United States,
Canada, or any other jurisdiction, is the sole responsibility of the
purchaser or reader.